MATT'S NOTO

Your guide to
one of Sicily's
greatest cities

Copyright © 2023 Matt Bird

Text & Photographs by Matt Bird

The moral right of the author has been asserted.

Apart from any fair dealing for the purposes of research or private study, or criticism or review, as permitted under Copyright, Deign and Patents Act 1998, this publication may only be reproduced, stored or transmitted, in any form or by any means, with prior permission in writing of the publishers, or in any case of the reprographic reproduction in accordance with the terms of licences issued by the Copyright Licensing Agency. Enquiries concerning reproduction outside these terms should be sent to the publishers.

Publish U Ltd
www.PublishU.com

All rights reserved.

THANKS

Big thanks to
Laurent Chaniac and Maria-Teresa Setaro-Chaniac
for inspiring me about Noto

INDEX

Welcome 7-9

Places to Visit 11-25

Beach Life 27-39

Wining & Dining 41-59

Snacking 61-65

Shopping 67-71

Slow Food 73-75

Vineyards 77-85

Art 87-95

Walks 97-101

Getting Around 103-107

Thank You 109

Noto Italy 111

WELCOME

Noto is one of the most beautiful cities in Europe. In my opinion, it is the jewel in the crown of the Mediterranean's largest island, Sicily. Dazzling sun and golden beaches and an unrivalled wealth of history and culture is topped off with world class food and wine.

Ancient Noto was destroyed by a devastating earthquake in 1693, leaving a blank canvas for the most prominent Baroque architects to rebuild the city in its current location. In 2002, Noto was awarded UNESCO world heritage status as 'representing the culmination and final flowering of baroque art in Europe'.

In downtown Noto you can visit the famous Cattedrale di San Nicolò di Mira as well as a plentiful supply of restaurants serving local cuisine from the sea and land. At all times of day and night, you can cool down with homemade Gelato, Cannoli and refreshing Granita and brioche.

The local beach is just a fifteen minute drive away with beautiful sand and clear blue sea. It is a wonderful place to spend the day swimming, reading and sleeping. Especially beautiful at sunset take a picnic blanket and a bottle of chilled wine for some super special moments.

In the surrounding area are many beaches, beach clubs, Michelin-star restaurants, vineyards, mountain walks with fresh water pools, places of interest and ancient historical sites to explore.

Congratulations on securing your copy of 'Noto Italy' which is regularly updated with recommendations of the latest places to visit, sights to see, and restaurants to dine in. All that you need for the perfect holiday!

PLACES TO VISIT

Noto lends its name to the surrounding area, Val di Noto, and a cluster of eight towns which, in 2002, were awarded UNESCO world heritage status.

The listed towns are:
Noto, Caltagirone, Militello in Val di Catania, Catania, Modica, Palazzolo Acreide, Ragusa and Scicli. These and many more local places provide all you need for a wonderful day out...

NOTO ANTICA: Fascinating Ruins

You can also visit the site and ruins of Noto Antica, or Ancient Noto, which were destroyed in 1693. As you walk through the city gates, follow the main path for 10 minutes and, as it turns to the left, you will come across a fascinating ruin of the city walls. There's also the floor of a house where you can imagine what life might have been like for those early Notoians. Take good walking shoes and plenty of water.

GPS: Noto Antica (20 minute drive)

MARZAMEMI: Seaside Town

A picturesque small seaside town renowned for tuna fishing and processing. Check out the two big stores known for their local specialities, including tuna and sun dried tomatoes: Adelfio Store and Campisi Store. It is also a lovely town to wander through for lunch at one of the alfresco restaurants in the Piazza, or go up market to Cortile Arabo a restaurant with an amazing terrace onto the Mediterranean. You will need to park on the outskirts of town and walk in.

GPS: Marzamemi (35 minute drive)

PALAZZOLO ACREDIE:
Arancino Central

A town with a lovely town square and known as a foodie spot with the famous Palazzolo Acreide sausage. In the south of the town, Corsino is known to serve the best arancino (small balls of rice filled with savoury filling coated in breadcrumbs and friend) in the region. It is home to the most fabulous rustic restaurant, Trattoria del Gallo which, as you enter, appears to be only a tiny street café. It specialises in Sicilian meat dishes, such as donkey. Palazzolo Acreide is home to the amazing Estro restaurant which, during the summer season, has a wonderful alfresco bar looking out to Mount Etna. On the outskirts of the city is a third century Akrai Greek Theatre, which is very much worth a visit.

GPS: Palazzolo Acredie (35 minute drive)

ORTIGIA, SIRACUSA: Island Life

The largest city in the region and considered the heart of Syracuse. The historic part of the city is on 'Ortigia Island' and connected by a bridge. The narrow streets, shops and wonderful restaurants make this an enchanting place to visit. There is also a spectacular cathedral in the main piazza and a Greek theatre. which is worth checking out on your way through. Ortigia is home to two restaurants of note: Cortile Spirito Santo, which is worthy of a Michelin star, and Don Camillo, which is also fabulous dining experience. Parking in Ortigia is very difficult for non-residents; I recommend parking at the Ortigia Palace Hotel and downloading the EasyPark App to pay for parking.

GPS: Ortigia Palace Hotel (45 minute drive)

RAGUSA IBLA: Simply Stunning

Ragusa Ibla is built on a limestone hill between two deep valleys, which creates spectacular views as you approach the city. Together with seven other cities in the Val di Noto, it is part of a UNESCO World Heritage Site. You can take a wonderful walk through the narrows streets, the gardens with a wonderful views and beautiful cathedral. It is home to the two-Michelin-star restaurant Duomo which, if you want to splash out, is well worth visiting. There are signs to a car park and I recommend using rather than trying to navigate the very narrow streets in your car.

GPS: Ragusa Ibla (60 minute drive)

TAORMINA: Hilltop Town

A breathtaking historic hilltop town dating back to before ancient Greece. It offers stunning views, winding lanes and wonderful places to experience typical Sicilian hospitality. You can visit the famous Greek amphitheatre, which is the second largest in Sicily after Syracuse. I love to step away from the bustle of the town to take a drink on the terrace of the Grand Hotel Timeo. Parking in Taormina is extremely challenging; I recommend putting the name of the following car park into your GPS.

GPS: Park Porta Catania, Corso Umberto 805 (105 minute drive)

MODICA: Chocolate Heaven

A UNESCO town en route to Ragusa that's famous for its chocolate. You can visit the chocolate museum, or even better, Bonajuto, the oldest chocolatier in Italy for a tour and tasting. There's also the more modern Sabadi chocolatier. Modica is also home to Accursio, a Michelin-starred restaurant. Park wherever you can!

GPS: Modica (40 minute drive)

VIVAI CUBA: House of Cacti

A fascinating cactus farm shipping cacti all over Europe and around the world. You can wander the shaded housing viewing hundreds of varieties of cacti of all shapes and sizes, small and large alike.

GPS: Vivai Cuba (20 minute drive)

NOTO CEMETERY: Open Air Museum

It may sound strange at first, but trust me, Noto's Cemetery, on the outskirts of town, is strangely beautiful. There are petite paupers graves and monumental mausoleums, for the rich, and something for everyone else in between. Take your time to walk between the rows and rows of graves, tombs and mausoleums in this open air museum.

GPS: Noto Cemetery (5 minute drive)

AGRIGENTO: Greek Architecture

Agrigento is known for the ruins of the ancient city of Akragas in the Valley of the Temples (it's actually on a hilltop), with some of the best Greek architecture in the world.

GPS: Agrigento Porta V (160 minute drive)

BEACH LIFE

The beaches along the South-East coast are some of the best in Sicily with clear turquoise water, beautiful sand and of an abundance of sun. Beaches are divided between the free ones with no amenities and those you pay, which are fully equipped and known as beach clubs.

When visiting a free beach, remember to take a parasol (which you can get from local shops for around €20) for protection from the intensity of the sun; high factor sun cream alone will not be sufficient. Drinking water is also essential.

Beach Clubs

Beach clubs are a great way to enjoy the sand and provide you with all the essentials. You have use of a parasol to protect you from the sun and comfy sun beds to bask in the sun, rest, sleep or read a book. There are bars for refreshments as well as showers and toilets. It is worth booking in advance, even if you phone on the morning as you head out.

The best time to go to the beaches, especially in high season, when they can be very busy, is early in the morning.

Eloro Camay Beach

This is our local beach and the closest to Noto. If you fancy a quick swim at any point in the day, or just a couple of hours of beach time, this is the spot. Street parking is free! Once parked up, you can either walk down the track by the side of the Hotel Club Eloro to what the locals call 'Eloro Camay Beach', or walk for 10 minutes over the hill to the old Eloro Beach.

GPS: Hotel Club Eloro (15 minute drive)

Marianelli Beach

A naturist beach, but not exclusively so. As you approach Marianelli, park in the field on the left just before the homestead. Parking in a local field costs a few euros and access to the nature costs a few euros per person. The beach is a 10 minute walk from the parking.

GPS: Marianelli (20 minute drive)

Calamosche Beach

A small and very popular beach in high season — it can get very crowded. Parking in a local field costs a few euros and then the beach is a 20 minute walk.

GPS: Calamosche (30 minute drive)

Agua Beach Club

A 'business class' beach club, providing you with a sun bed and parasol. Using their smartphone app, you can order refreshments to be delivered to you. It costs around €15 per person for a sun bed. Parking is extra.

GPS: Agua Beach Club (30 minute drive)

Noto Beach Club

A 'first class beach club' providing you with a luxury sunbed and parasol. The friendly team serves you refreshments at your sunbed through the day. Owned by the five-star Il San Corrado di Noto Hotel, you can expect a high standard. It costs €70 but for an amazing day of being indulged, it's worth it. Parking is included.

GPS: Noto Beach Club (15 minute drive)

WINING & DINING

Sicily is well known in Italy and beyond for its amazing food and wine. Being by the coast, you can expect plenty of fresh fish and, being Italy, lots of pasta and meat choices, too. Given the climate, most restaurants offer alfresco dining, which creates a stunning experience. Dining times vary from country to country, Sicily is classically Mediterranean, which means people tend to only head out for dinner later in the evening, typically 8.30pm onwards.

You will need to make a table reservation in advance. Pop in or Google their telephone number and give them a call to make your reservation. Restaurants are used to international English speaking guests so you shouldn't have any trouble being understood.

Neighbourhood

Noto has a lot of neighbourhood restaurants to choose from.

Norma's Bistro

An all day super friendly bistro. Ask for Norma.

(Via Rocco Pirri)

Dammuso

Run by the brother and mother of Crocifisso Chef Marco Baglieri. Ask for Andrea.

(Via Rocco Pirri)

Retablo

Located in a discrete courtyard downtown.
Ask for Katharina.

(Via Alfredo Baccarini 4/6)

Vicolo

Specialising in fish. Ask for Chef Aurelio.

(Off Principe Umberto on Vico Milazzo 9)

Casa Matta

Reputed to be the best pizza in central Noto.

(Via Tommaso Fazello 23)

Nache

A lovely family run restaurant with alfresco dining (and a few tables inside). Love that they have a turntable and play vinyls whilst you dine.

(Via Pier Capponi 4)

Geranio

Fabulous for pizza but also the specialities of the day are a winner.

(Via Ducezio 33)

Al Vecchio Molo 'The Old Peer'

A very understated fish restaurant by a village fishing harbour at Calabernardo.

GPS: Calabernardo (15 min drive)

Live Music

Noto has a small but growing live music scene with local churches hosting classic concerts and bars and casual restaurants music. My two favourite spots are:

Cavour Lounge

Fridays, Saturdays and Sundays are big at Cavour with live music guaranteeing the venue is full and overflowing onto the street.

(Via Camillo Benso di Cavour 86)

Secret Eat Drink Stay

On live music nights, the crowd overflows onto the stairs immediately outside the restaurant.

(On the staircase of Via Fratelli Bandiera)

Rustic

If you are open to rustic eating - which I would describe as simple Sicilian cuisine often in a shabby setting - try these:

Kuchnir Domowa 'Home Kitchen'

Imagine a large lean-to on the side of a rural house. The menu is literally homestead to table with a pen of black pigs outside and produce from the garden.

GPS: En route to Cava Grande (40 minute drive)

Casa Rossa 'Red House'

Everybody who is anybody in Noto hangs out at this rustic restaurant on the outskirts of town.

GPS: Casa Rossa (5 min drive)

Fine Dining

Noto and the surrounding area has an increasing number of fine dining experiences. If, like me, you are a foodie or just like a special meal, then you are in for a treat. They all offer tasting menus providing the chef the opportunity to show off a combination of seasonal local ingredients and their particular passion.

- Cortile Spirito Santo, Siracusa Ortigia
  (Chef Giuseppe Torrisi)
- Estro, Palazzolo Acreide
  (Chef Giuseppe Luparelli)
- Crocifisso, Noto
  (Chef Marco Baglieri)
- Accursio*, Modica
  (Chef Accursio Craparo)
- Villadorata Country House, Noto
  (Chef Viviana Varese)
- Cortile Arabo, Marzamemi
  (Chef Massimo Giaquinta)
- Duomo**, Ragusa Ibla
  (Chef Ciccio Sultano)

At these restaurants, it is absolutely essential to make table reservations well in advance. In the peak season, that's weeks ahead.

SNACKING

My experience is that the hotter the climate the less hungry I feel, so snacking is the order of the day.

As you explore Noto, it is hard not to notice the Sicilian love for Gelato (Italian ice cream) and on a hot day it is very welcome! There is also the infamous Granita made from ice, sugar and fruit, which is classically enjoyed with a fresh brioche roll. These are made throughout the day and are sometimes served hot from the oven. They are served from breakfast through to dinner, so anytime you wish.

Granita & Gelato

Mangiafico

In my opinion, this offers Noto's best Granita and Gelato, but try as many as your visit allows and let me know what you think!

(Via Ducezio 2)

Cafe Sicilia

This is a destination for many visitors to Noto, located near the cathedral with inside seatingas well as alfresco space, with guests spilling out on the street.

(Corso Vittorio Emanuele 125)

Pasticceria Kennedy

Located in Noto alta, this is conveniently moments from the apartment and is perfect to pick up something to enjoy on the balcony or terrace.

(Principe Umberto 128)

Pizza

Maidda Bakery

Maidda Bakery is famous for breads made from ancient Sicilian grains and each day offers various bread pizza. They are great if you fancy a snack or grab-and-go lunch. There are no meat options but they still taste fabulous.

(Via Ducezio 85)

Aperitivo Culture

Italy has a wonderful aperitivo culture of generosity and hospitality. When you arrive at a restaurant ask for an 'aperitivo' a starter drink of your choice. Spritz (Aperol, prosecco and soda water) is perhaps the most common aperitivo. Together with your drink, you will be served a complimentary plate of snacks. This is on offer whether you are dining at the restaurant or not.

The most scenic locations for aperitivo is the Gagliardi Boutique Hotel rooftop, which has stunning panoramic views of the city especially at sunset. You need to book for aperitivo via the hotel. It is open from 7pm

(Via Silvio Spaventa 41)

Enjoy trying out the local aperitivo, it's a great way to unwind, experience the local culture and soak up the atmosphere after a day at the beach or sightseeing. Once you have found your favourite spot remember to let me know and I'll tell you mine.

SHOPPING

Eating out in Sicily does not need to be expensive but you might wish to cook the odd meal at home.

The closest supermarket to Noto alta is a 'Coop' which has a good range of products.

From Via Principe Umberto, walk down Via Bernardino Grimaldi, and at the end — on the right — you will find steps down to a small car park behind the Coop.

GPS: Via Enrico Amante 1 (3 minute walk)

Food

If you would like a bigger supermarket, there are lots of choices if you are happy to jump in the car. The supermarket, with a very extensive range, can be found at a shopping centre on the road to Avola. It's worth the short drive to find every ingredient you can imagine.

GPS: Centro Commerciale Il Giardino (15 minute drive)

Wine

Sicily is Italy's largest wine producing region, and thanks to Mount Etna, creating a volcanic terroir the wines can be of incredible minerality. The local place to buy your wines for aperitivos and meals is at 'D&T Bevande'. You can park in the street outside and walk over. Do not be fooled by the warehouse-like appearance of the supplier; once you walk towards the back of the premises you will find a temperature-controlled wine room full of delightful wines at incredible value!

GPS: Via Gaetano Salvemini 100 (5 minute drive)

Olive Oil

The Ruta family have been making olive oil in Sicily for more than half a century and they produce award winning olive oils. Visiting their farm is a treat because you can get to taste their full range of olive oils, like you would taste wines — it's amazing! Check out their English website at...   https://frantoioruta.com/en

GPS: C. da Cozzo Scozzaria, Castelluccio (25 minute drive)

Almonds

Sicily's almonds are particularly rich in aroma and flavour and mostly grown in Noto, Avola and the province of Siracusa. So, if you like almonds, even if just a little, I recommend getting yourself a bag or two. The best place is a family producer, Pagliarello. They choose to maintain old machinery at significant expense because they think it takes better care of the almonds.

GPS: Via Roma 71   (5 minute drive)

Fish

In Noto alta, we have an incredible fishmongers, just a few minutes' walk from the apartment. So if you are up for some home cooking, head over to La Pescheria Ristorante E Pescheria Da Spugnetti Sebastiano in the morning and see what has been caught that day. You will be amazed at the quality and value for money.

GPS: Via Rosolino Pilo 20   (5 minute walk)

Roadside Stalls

As you drive through Noto you will see roadside stalls selling all sorts of fresh produce, including the famous Pachino (30 minute drive) tomatoes which taste like nothing you will find elsewhere. If there is anything you like the look of pull over and buy some. Pay in cash and don't expect a receipt.

Sicilia Handmade

A boutique of leather goodies where they will also make to order.

(Via Ruggero Settimo 18)

A'mare Noto

A beautiful clothing and accessories concept store. Ask for Monica.

(Corso Vittorio Emanuele 43)

Spazio Noto

A small art gallery of art, photography, sculpture and design. Ask for Paolo.

(Via Rocco Pirri 32)

SLOW FOOD

Slow food is a movement that was founded in Italy in 1986 by the international campaigner Carlo Petrini, promoting local sustainable food producers. It strives to preserve traditional and regional cuisine and encouraging the farming of seeds, plants and livestock characteristic of the local ecosystem.

Ispica Sesame

Thanks to its abundant water, Ispica is an important agricultural centre. Sesame was introduced during the time of Arab rule. The harvest is graduated so must be repeated several times and then the crop is cleaned through sieves.

Noto Almond

Harvest takes place in July and August with workers called 'ciurme' who beat the branches with long canes and collect the almonds on large cloths spread on the ground. The almonds are then bagged and hulled.

Palazzolo Acreide Sausage

Palazzolo Acreide is known for its long tradition of pork curing, dating back to the Roman era when each family would travel with pigs and goats to ensure they always had meat and milk. Sausages were always prized because they could be cooked fresh or dried for later. The Palazzolo Acreide has nine cuts of meat: the neck and jowl, lard, collar, loin, shoulder, trotter, underbelly, leg and fat (no more than 25%). The only other ingredients added are Sicilian sea salt, chilli pepper, wild fennel, from the Iblei Mountains, and red wine from the Noto Valley.

Image Credit: italianfoodexcellence.com

Leonforte Peaches in a Bag

Each year in June, something crazy happens: the farmers place little sacks of vellum on the green peaches one at a time. Theses bags protect the peaches from parasites and the wind and can be harvested at the last minute.

Nebrodi Black Pig

These pigs are medium to small in size and have a black coat with stiff bristles forming a small mane down their back. They are raised in semi-wild conditions in the forests and meadows of the Nebrodi Mountains and only given 'zimme' (small huts) when essential.

Giarratana Onion

Giarratana, in the Iblei Mountains, produces extraordinary sweet onions. The bulbs have a slightly squashed shape and brownish-white skin. After harvesting, the bulbs are left to dry in the fields for a week and then stored in dry, airy rooms.

VINEYARDS

Sicily is Italy's primary wine-producing region with a number of unique indigenous grape varietals. The most produced reds are Nero d'Avola, Frappato and Nerello Mascalese, and whites Catarratto, Grillo and Inzolia. My experience is that the wines of Sicily have great acidity and minerality, which I'm sure is in part due to the volcanic terroir. Being so close to so many vineyards provides an opportunity to visit, my recommendations are:

Planeta

One of the three largest wine producers in Sicily. The 'Viagglo Nella DOC Noto' tour which walks you around the estate learning about the Planeta story and tasting their wines as you go is highly recommended. The tour culminates in an aperitivo and snacks. There is a cost of €45 per person.

Telephone: +39 925 1955460

GPS: Planeta Noto, Contrada Coda Finocchio (20 minute drive)

Cos

An organic winery founded in 1980 and now producing some of Sicily's best wines. Their 'Pithos' (the Greek word for a large earthware jar) wines are fermented in large clay pots in the ground. Well worth a visit and a tasting.

Telephone: +39 932 876145

GPS: S.P. 3 Acate-Chiaramonte, 97019 Vittoria (110 minute drive)

Marabino

A relatively unknown producer making an array of stunning organic wines from local grape varietals. It is worth phoning ahead to book a tasting of their range of wines.

Telephone: +39 335 5284101

GPS: Societa' Agricola Marabino (30 minute drive)

Terrasol

A small producer of natural wines and well worth popping by the cellar door to pick up some wines to enjoy at home. Their traditional method sparkling wine the Mandala - dry and made from 100% chardonnay - is highly recommended.

Telephone: +39 093 2901081

GPS: Cantina Terrasol Winery (30 minute drive)

Winery visits are only possible with a reservation.

ART

Noto is bursting with art and creativity. The city has some of the finest Sicilian architecture, street art and installations, galleries and art exhibitions, private studios and events, not to mention the famous Infiorata di Noto, when the streets are laid with flower petals.

Street Art

There are three staircases which take you from downtown Noto to Noto alta and each has beautiful step art

Via Mariannina Coffa,

Via Fratelli Bandiera and

Via Dante Alighieri

Baroque Architecture

Noto is well known as the baroque capital of Sicily. Walk the streets and check out the facades, and particularly balconies, around the city. Some of the best examples can be found on

Via Corrado Nicolaci

Galleries

There is a constant stream of art exhibitions in local galleries and a stroll around downtown Noto will reveal most of these locations.

Private Studios

One of my favourite local artists is Sergio Fiorentino who I have found to be very open to opening his studio to visitors.

Contact him via his Instagram @sergiofiorentino

Events

The Infiorata di Noto is the towns famous annual flower festival (middle of May) when streets are lined with works of art made from colourful flower petals.

Via Nicolaci

WALKS

As an introduction to the city, I recommend walking along Corso Vittorio Emanuele (the main street) from East to West, starting at the far end of Piazza Luigi Adorno.

'Downtown' Noto

San Corrado
Across the road from the eastern end of the Corso is a statue of Corrado, the patron protector of Noto. Standing here and looking east, you can see the sea.

Arco di Trionfo
The city gate, like much of the city, is made of limestone which appears in different shades of colour as the sun reflects on it through the day.

Noto Cathedral
The Church of St Nicholas sits at the top of a monumental staircase. The cathedral began to be rebuilt here soon after the earthquake but was not completed until 1776.

Palazzo Ducezio
The palace is opposite the cathedral and currently is home of the town hall. You can pay €2 to access the first floor terrace that has some views of Noto.

Palazzo Nicolaci di Villadorata
After the Cathedral, turn right up Via Corrado Nicolaci and you will see the palace on the left, with its stunning baroque balconies.

San Carlo
Returning to the main street walking west immediately on the left, you will see a building entrance with a red carpet outside. This is San Carlo, where you can pay €2 and access the rooftop via a narrow spiral staircase, which offers the best panoramic views of Noto.

Hiking & Fresh Water Swimming

Turning away from the coast, Noto is surrounded by stunning mountains and canyons. If you would like a strenuous walk, and at the other end swim in stunning fresh water pools, there are two that I would recommend:

Cava del Carosello

Located off of Noto Antica (the ancient city of Noto). Park by the main entrance and walk for 10 minutes along the main track until you see paths on the right. There are several paths you can take that will lead you to a wire fence, follow the fence until you reach some green gates, which will take you down to the pools. Do not be tempted to cross the stiles on the wire fence!

GPS: Noto Antica (35 minute drive)

Cava Grande

Located on the other side of the valley, you will need a few euros to pay the local farmer to park in his field. Walk up and over the hill following track B for 40 minutes.

GPS: Cavagrande (40 minute drive)

GETTING AROUND

In order to fully enjoy Sicily you need wheels!

Car Hire

The easiest, cheapest and most convenient way to do this is to hire a car at the airport. I regularly use Italy car hire company Noleggiare and would recommend them. You can email them directly at **catania@noleggiare.it**

I would strongly recommend you pay for the premium insurance with zero excess in case of accidents. Sicily is full of narrow streets and bumps and scratches happen! It is best not to pay for the premium insurance online, as you will pay more and it will not be zero excess. Wait until you pick-up your car and pay for it then, you will get a much better price.

Top Tips

1. In Italy it is the law to drive with your licence on your person. Not doing so can lead to an unwanted fine, so best to keep your driving license in your pocket.

2. When it comes to packing your hand luggage, include a smartphone to USB lead. You will be able to use this to connect your smartphone and its GPS to the car's navigation screen. This means you can keep your eyes on the road and the dashboard rather than looking down at the screen of your phone.

3. As you would in any country when you leave the car ensure that anything of value is out of sight.

4. Most car hire firms will ask you to return the car with a full tank of petrol. When you turn off the main dual carriageway (E45) towards the airport — onto another dual carriageway the Strada Provinciale (701) — you will see two petrol stations before you take the next road to the airport. These are the most convenient places to fill up.

5. As you arrive at the airport, it can be confusing about where to go to return your hire car. I always head to car zone P4, after which you will see more specific signs for your car rental company.

6. If you need to go to the airport to pick up friends or take a bus from there to another part of the island, you can park in your rental company's parking area for free. Just mention to them what you are doing and how long you will be — whether hours or days — and they will be only too happy. Please note, you are unable to park a rental car in the other car parks at the airport.
7. There is lots of free street parking in Sicily but always check to be sure.

Taxi

If you want to go out of town for dinner and enjoy more than a glass of wine, you may want to use a taxi.

Noto does not have Uber or a 'local taxi firm', just lots of independents. So, if you want a taxi you are going to need to ask around. If one of them says they can't help you ask them for the name and number of someone else. It's best to contact them via WhatsApp. If you would like a couple of numbers to get you started please email me.

THANK YOU

I hope you love Noto and the surrounding area as much as I do. Please let me know about any other little gems you discover during your time here so that I can add to this travel guide for the benefit of others.

Feel the love,
Matt

Matt@NotoItaly.com

REST

To enquire about holiday homes
in Noto please

Contact Matt...

Email **Matt@NotoItaly.com**
WhatsApp **+44 7444 111222**

INVEST

Are you interested in resting or investing in Noto, Italy?

Noto Italy Ltd offers the inside track on local holiday rental investment opportunities.

Contact Matt or Giuseppe...

Email **matt@NotoItaly.com**
or **giuseppe@NotoItaly.com**

WhatsApp **+447444 111222**
or **+39333 4264337**

Instagram @NotoItaly
www.NotoItaly.com

Printed in Great Britain
by Amazon